<u>Title</u>: Notions on Emotions

<u>Author</u>: Nick del Castillo

<u>Illustrator</u>: Elena "Nelly" del Castillo

<u>Other books by Nick</u>:

"Virtues to Happiness" © 2016
"From Zero to Success!" © 2017
"The Seven Signs of Charisma" © 2021

<u>Dedication</u>:

This book is dedicated to the Wisdom Family.

Kindle Direct Publishing, 2nd Edition © 2024

<u>Foreword</u>: by Will Wisdom

I laughed with glee when Nick told me his next project was going to be a book called, "Notions on Emotions." This is because emotions are a topic I am also interested in, a fascinating aspect to what makes us human.

"Whooaah! Sometimes, I get a good feeling! Yeah. Get a feeling like I never ever ever knew I had before, yeah, I get a good feeling, yeah!" ~Avicii (using the voice of Etta James),

LE7ELS

In life we can experience some amazing highs, and some amazing lows. The heart of man runs deep, deeper than the ocean. Emotions are a tricky topic. On the one hand, good and bad feelings can be an indication of whether or not we are doing the right thing. On the other hand, emotions can often be deceiving, leading us to do things and say things we might later regret. In this case the old adage, "mind over matter" applies. That said, sometimes in life calculation gets in the way, and it's best to follow our heart.

We're all human and have our weaknesses. What's important is that we keep trying. The relationship between the mind and the heart is a profound mystery. We will probably never be able to understand it completely. However, in the end I believe that the mind and the heart can and will be completely satisfied and at peace.

Nick is a very insightful and virtuous friend of mine, and I know he has some powerful emotions, as I do. I can't wait to read what he has to say in this book. So, put on your lotions, we're going to go swim in the oceans and gain some notions on emotions! *Bonne Chance! Will Wisdom*

Prologue:

From "Virtues to Happiness" Chapter 24:

"24. <u>Tranquility</u>:

Tranquility is [the] peacefulness of the mind and heart. It comes as a result of having violently fought against the vices and is a relative of the virtue of temperance (self-control).

Five Ways to Live Tranquility:

If you are angry at someone[,] wait a few hours or even days before speaking to the person. Never act on pure emotion or in the heat of the moment. You will regret it later.

In the face of danger, succumbing to nervousness or fear will only make things worse. It is easier said than done, but when calm, it will be easier to think logically and enable oneself to make a decision with greater clarity and finesse.

When life is tough and you are down in the dumps, take a few moments to reflect on the positive aspects of your life. Know that there is always the opportunity for things to get better. If you reflect on this, you will be more at ease and will be fostering the virtue of hope.

Trying to understand the others...their personalities, backgrounds, moods etc. will help you to be more tranquil and forgiving. Oftentimes we judge too quickly or do not give other people a chance to be known or understood. Being calm and tranquil amidst war and violence are effective weapons to win people's hearts. Having the inner strength to be at peace can make us effective in leading by example."

Table of Contents

1. <u>What are Emotions?</u>

What do you FEEL? Be honest, do you really know? If so, do you know how to deal with what you feel? We as human beings are so good at understanding and observing things that are outside ourselves, yet the most challenging things to decipher are actually within ourselves. On a practical level, we have been able to subdue the earth and provide advancements in the fields of medicine and technology, but to this day we still struggle with the same emotional problems as that of our ancestors. Life is generally simple, but we ourselves are the ones that make it complicated. Life becomes complex when we seek out our comfort zone and succumb to easy escapes. Life becomes simpler when we decide to tackle difficult decisions that come our way. We cannot avoid making decisions. Even deciding not to act is a decision in itself. Many times our emotions play a key role in our everyday plans. Emotions are feelings that have the power to drive our thoughts, words and actions.

Not everything we feel like doing should be done and at the same time not everything we feel is something we should ignore. Having feelings is what makes us human, but if they are not guided by our reason then they can be very destructive. The problem with the 'I feel' mentality is that it can be very selfish at times. People with that type of 'modus operandi' can become a slave to their whims and never really progress in life. 'One day I'll decide to go to work, one day I won't' will not make a good employee. No one likes to be around a fickle person. However, there is a balance. Sometimes we need to focus on ourselves in order to address a particular problem, but most of the time we are happiest when we do not think too much about ourselves.

That is why people with big egos get hurt so easily. It is because they are constantly thinking about themselves which is the swamp that they create for themselves and continually live in. If you are not happy, go and make someone else happy and the happiness will return to you like a boomerang.

Emotions are here to stay and they are part of our human nature, but we also have the ability to display logic and to reason things out. The dynamic balance between the two can be tricky at times, but they need that balance as two wings on an airplane are needed in order for the aircraft to fly. Self-knowledge is key in order to channel our emotions. Knowing oneself can be tricky at times, but knowing our patterns and tendencies can help us to anticipate tribulations within ourselves. Emotions are like fire. That fire inside of us can be very easily ignited. We cannot escape the heat of the fire. We must either extinguish the fire or somehow channel the flames. Fire can cook food and keep you warm,

but it can also destroy your wooden spindle table and even

burn you! The worst option we can do is to lock it up inside.

Every energy needs an outlet, especially ones that come

within us which are our passions and feelings.

2. <u>Logical vs. Emotional</u>

Two main schools of thought when it comes to making decisions boil down to 'logical' and 'emotional' decision making. The third school is in a sense like a wide spectrum which includes everything in-between. We need to examine ourselves and see where we lean towards. If we are overly logical we should remember that deep down inside we have feelings and other people have them as well. If we are overly emotional we should remember our reasonable side and that we are creatures that can think and solve problems. People who are logical have the advantage of being efficient and practical, but may lack the human side of things which include empathy and compassion. An overly logical person may even seem a bit robotic and somewhat unhuman. On the other hand, someone who is overly emotional may be able to connect well with people and be socially savvy, but can potentially have plans that fail, due to poor planning, or because of the lack of logical thinking. Those that do not have self-control can be seen as more animalistic in the sense that they just go with their instincts and feelings without any regard for other people and the moral implications of their actions. All 'heart' and no 'brains' can be a recipe for disaster, but all 'brains' and no 'heart' makes us lifeless. At the end of the day, we should seek out the truth in every situation we are in and understand the bigger picture.

Do not fight on emotion, but when fighting put your emotion into it. Have a plan and then take action to execute it. If you are at a crossroads between two choices and one of them looks great on paper, but you have a gut feeling it is not going to work or have a hunch something is not right, then look into it. It would not be good to go immediately with your gut feeling, but at the same time do not ignore it. Try to go a little further as to why? The reverse is true. For example, if it feels right and you are filled with joy that is great, but look into logic and reason and see if your decision is possible or even worth doing. Having a great idea can be a nice inspiration that came from your feelings, but it will take planning and perspiration to get it done. Our decision making comes down to the degree of our trust and the extent of our need.

If a transportation company is offering a bus service from New York to Chicago, but you do not believe the service is reliable or if you do not trust the company then you probably will not buy the ticket. Another scenario is if you do believe that the service is reputable and trustworthy, but have no need, then it will not result in a purchase. How you decide if the service is trustworthy may be based on feelings, reasons or a mix of the two. Someone can argue that the salesperson built good rapport and made them feel at ease or even good about themselves and this resulted in the purchase. Another person can argue that the salesperson showed them that they were better priced than their competitors and have a flect of brand new buses and that also resulted in the purchase of the ticket. Either way, whether your decision was more based on feelings or reasons, both people concluded to trust the business and take the service. How we think and make decisions can be shaped over time depending on various factors and is something that overlaps with the mystery of our personality.

3. <u>Personality & Emotions</u>

The word 'personality' can be difficult to define. According to Merriam Webster's online application, personality is defined as "the complex of characteristics that distinguishes an individual or a nation or group especially: the totality of an individual's behavioral and emotional characteristics". Although defining what personality is can be both a philosophical and a semantic challenge, let us take the angle of defining 'personality' as consistent patterns in a person's behavior that capture the essence of a particular individual. There are many different types of people. Truth be told, since each person is complex and no two people are exactly the same, it can be said that there are literally billions of different personalities. Psychologists and other professionals have attempted to categorize different personalities, whether it is in the Myers-Briggs 16 personalities, the four temperaments, etc. Each classification system has its pluses and minuses like everything else. For example, take labeling two people as the ENFJ (extroverted, intuitive, feeling and judging) personality type. Each person may fall into the same personality bucket, but may be very different due to other social or emotional factors. Someone who is categorized as an ISTP (introverted, sensing, thinking and prospecting) may not necessarily be the complete opposite of an ENFJ. Two people that are labeled as choleric/sanguine may exhibit different personalities from each other as well. Even knowing oneself is a lifelong mystery in which we can know more and more but we will never fully know ourselves or other people. There are predictive patterns, yet given the complexity of being human, each person is in a sense unpredictable, unique and therefore irreplaceable. Someone who is consistently 'the life of the party' may be that of a sanguine personality, but someone who is consistently 'laid back and chill' may be that of a phlegmatic personality type. Personality overlaps with emotions. Each personality type has its particular strengths, weaknesses and its emotional idiosyncrasies. Honing our character and accepting our personality is a lifelong struggle. Each personality is good, but everyone could use refinement to smooth off the rough edges. For example, someone may overreact to the smallest thing, whereas another person might be too passive and lazy. Each personality type has their natural dispositions when it comes to their emotions. Emotions can be used for good or for bad purposes depending on how we direct them. The key phrase in the former sentence is 'direct them'. Having a certain feeling is not as important as to how you direct it. Someone may be naturally inclined to taking action and leading a charge, as characteristic of that in a choleric person. Another person may be more inclined to study in an orderly and methodical manner, as that of a melancholic person. Whatever personality we have, we should build on our strengths and to try to overcome our weaknesses. Even though we may continually mess up or fail in being overly angry, excessively sentimental etc., we should not get bogged down by that and just move forward. We should be like a long and winding river. If the water keeps flowing there is freshness and vitality. If the water slows down or stands still then stagnation occurs, which can turn the water into a nasty swamp. At times we get down and feel we are trapped and think that no one understands us. Sometimes deciphering emotions can be as tricky as trying to diffuse a bomb that is connected to hundreds of tangled wires.

4. <u>Emotional Interpretations</u>

People who are going through a hard time may be able to relate to other people that have faced similar emotions or shocking experiences, yet each person is not affected in exactly the same manner. When dealing with emotions it would be inaccurate to say 'I know what you are going though.' We have an idea and sometimes even a very good idea of what is going on, but never a perfect representation. A visual example would be that of clothing. Each person has a specific height and weight and particular proportions with our arms and legs. A clothing store owner may be somewhat accurate as to whether you are a small, medium or large, but it will never be as accurate as that of a custom-made suit done by a high-end tailor.

Everyone is different. Each person is affected by the complexity of their own emotions in various ways. However, there are some people who have special gifts in being able to 'read' emotions. Although people cannot read thoughts, sometimes people's feelings can be read from their facial expressions, tone of voice and body language. Some people have a knack for this or possess the gift of intuition for being able to know what someone is feeling, whereas some may be more aloof. Coining new terms, there are objective emotional interpretations (OEI) and subjective emotional interpretations (SEI). In OEI, one interprets other people's emotions based on human patterns and studies that show consistent results when analyzing similar cases. SEI understands patterns particular to the individual. Some idiosyncrasies might be particular to specific people. To get to know someone can take a very long time. That is why people flock to their family and close friends when they need someone to talk to for advice, since they know them

better than others. Sometimes our feelings do not remain on

the surface but sink into the depths of our being.

5. <u>Repressed Feelings</u>

Repressed feelings can sometimes overlap as the proverbial 'skeletons in the closet.' There are two types of repressed feelings: conscious and unconscious. If we experience a very particular hurt that is the direct cause of our unpleasant feelings then it can be said to be conscious. If we somehow feel hurt, but do not know exactly why, there could be a wide range of reasons. One of them could be a hurt in our lives that we have decided to ignore since it was so embarrassing and painful and we have somehow managed to get over it, but the remnants linger on like a useless vestige in the body or as in the faint markings from an erased pencil sketch. Most of it is gone, but the trace remains in our subconscious mind. These types of repressed feelings are unconscious. Sometimes revisiting an occurrence in our lives can cause a lot of pain, but knowing and accepting our reality can actually set us free. We should not revisit the past so we can feel miserable or wallow in the murky seas of self-pity, but so that we can learn, grow and have a better understanding of our past. We often like to have reasons as to why things happen or do not happen. Sometimes pinpointing why we feel hurt is not so easy. The physical realm has its enigmas and challenges, but these are a lot easier to address than in the psychological realm. For example, if someone's leg hurts, knowing what the cause is will not necessarily cure the pain, but knowing what it is may help in treating the pain. The pain may be from a bruise, a cut, a sprain or even a broken bone. In the psychological realm there may be overlapping factors that dynamically interplay in and with our environment. Pinpointing the cause is not obvious and sometimes can be quite complex. If the cause is unknown for one's psychological hurt then it is best to acknowledge the pain and then to simply let it go. To let go does not mean to just 'let it go' since in thinking of letting it go we do not actually let it go, but ironically keep thinking about it. If someone says, 'do not think of a cantaloupe' then we will probably think of a cantaloupe now that it was mentioned. The best way to let things go are in the following ways:

1. Focus on the task at hand: Be totally present in that conversation with your friend. Focus on the paddle ball game being played. Delve into your model airplane hobby.

2. Have a set and semi-tight schedule: The more time we have, the more time we have to waste, so use it wisely. Flow and productivity will naturally drown out all the distractions in so far as we have a laser-like focus with specific goals.

3. Socialize: When we spend time with family and friends we take the focus away from ourselves. Listening to other people can be therapeutic.

Our emotions are very powerful and they cannot be turned off like in the flip of a switch. We need to take time for them to cool down. If we have feelings that we have not addressed then it can take courage to face them, but if we do address them, we will be liberated. It boils down to knowing ourselves, accepting our condition and then moving on by a great focus on the task at hand and not thinking too much about ourselves. Doing so can lead to the development of insecurities.

6. <u>Insecurities</u>

We all have insecurities to one degree or another. Oftentimes we feel the need to show off or to brag about something in order to be liked. The initial spark that caused the insecurity can be bad and acting on it is when it becomes worse. No one really cares about you showing off about you except you, and the fact of the matter is that you should not either. The initial feeling of wanting to be liked is not bad, but it can be if it is at the cost of goodness and truth. There is nothing wrong with being a likeable person, but we should not seek it out. People will catch on sooner or later if someone is a sincere person or not. If we are insecure, then it means we are holding on to something that we should not be holding on to. We will never be free from our emotions, but we can be free when we do not give them free reign. If people know we like to be liked then we can become easily manipulated. Once a weakness is known the entry point of attack becomes more obvious than the sun in the sky. The reasons people are insecure are the following:

1. Past failures (Once bitten, twice shy)

2. Lack of confidence (Low self-esteem, low confidence)

3. Fear of what the others may think (Avoiding pain)

4. Do not want to look bad (Excessive self love)

If you are insecure, face your fear and do what is right. It may be painful at first, but it is more painful to live in fear and in doubt. We need to be honest with ourselves and not lock things up inside.

7. <u>Passive Aggressiveness</u>

Pow! Bang! Smack! Lots of noise and chaos. It may be rough, but at least you know why and where the noise is coming from. In that situation you can at least attempt to address what is directly attacking you. Imagine a situation where you have peace and quiet among a group of people, but then one of them suddenly strikes you from a hidden corner. You look to turn around and they vanish amidst the crowd and then later on you get struck again from your blindside. Amongst the people you seemingly have no enemies, but the hidden, backhanded actions tell otherwise. Sometimes we can have feelings or even act on being passive aggressive. A fundamental sign of being passive aggressive is putting on a plastic smile for another person but burning with anger on the inside and subtly attempting to hurt the other person. Some reasons we can have this emotion are the following:

1. We are afraid to speak our mind in fear of retaliation.

2. We want to look good in front of others.

3. We prefer to be sneaky rather than confrontational.

If there is hidden anger we should address it immediately lest it should grow worse. Storing up hurts is like collecting sticks of dynamite in a clandestine closet. Nothing is ever a problem until a spark sets off the batch and then ... kaboom! Let it not lead to future traumas.

8. <u>Traumas</u>

There is no doubt that there can be people that suffer from traumas their entire lives, as a scar may become a permanent facial feature. The scar is not the problem but our relationship with it. Agreed that sometimes facing traumas can be overwhelming to the point where counseling and medical help are needed, but when these fall short or have limited effects is when we need to change how we view our traumas. It is not in changing our past that we break free, but in changing our attitude towards our past. Paraphrasing Anita Moorjani's book, "Dying to Be Me": If I ask you right now to scan the room you are in and look around for all the items in the room that are 'red' and then I ask you to close your eyes shut and now tell me everything in the room that is 'blue', then needless to say you will have a hard time naming anything that is 'blue'... why? Because you were not focused on it. Oftentimes we get what we decide to focus on. If you focus on the ugly part of the picture you may have an unpleasant experience; if you focus on the beautiful part of it then you may have a pleasant experience. Yes, willpower is important, but it is not brute mental strength which will necessarily get us through.

What is needed are directed actions that shift our focus toward what is good. As Steven Covey referred to in "First Things First" we need to have a sense of where our true north is and to examine if our ladder is leaning on the right house. What is the point of climbing the ladder if the end result is not wanted? Where are we ultimately headed in the midst of all our thoughts and actions? We can spend the rest of our lives trapped by a trauma or we can break free by focusing on what we can do to help ourselves and the people around us. If you accept what you cannot change and change what you can, then you are on the way to becoming a happier person. There are people who have everything going for them in terms of wealth, health and fame, but are outright miserable. There are people on the opposite end of the spectrum that have nothing going for them, and yet they are very happy. Why? The reason for this phenomenon is because they knew how to focus on the positive. It goes back to the adage of 'life isn't what happens to you, but what you do with what happens.' The ones that do not succeed in doing this are those that are locked in a hamster wheel. They keep running and running, but never advance further. In other words, they put in a lot of effort, but do not move ahead. We should avoid looking back as we would to avoid a dangerous precipice or if we were at the edge of a cliff. Let us not keep revisiting things over and over again with no return on our emotional investments.

9. <u>Rumination</u>

Let's see that again and again ... and again. We often like to replay events that are recorded on videos, and even if they are unrecorded we replay them in our minds. It makes logical sense to replay the good times, but why do we also replay the bad times? Sometimes it is hard to let go of the past. Even though it is hard, it is a lot more painful to hold on than it is to let go. Imagine trying to hold on to a falling rope that is attached to an anvil. It is better to let go and avoid rope burn than it is to hold on. Sometimes we hold on with the false illusion that we can change the past or feel better by recalling the incident. When someone says 'just let go' it is easier said than done. The reason being is that it psychologically 'itches'. It is hard to ignore the itchy mental feeling and you just want to 'scratch' it. If you give in to the impulse and scratch it you will bleed and not let the wound heal. Trick the mind into challenging the emotion into positive outlets. It goes back to focusing and then taking action. We often get what we decide to focus on. Holding on to the past and reliving it can spark the same emotions as when we were hurt for the first time. If we do, then we have what is called 'resentment', which etymologically comes from the prefix 're' (again, repeat) and the Latin word 'sentire' (to feel), which means 'feeling again'. Why hold on to a painful feeling?

Holding on to the past is like a rock climber with a huge backpack full of useless stuff. It does not seem to be a big deal until the climber slips and then luckily holds on to a branch to save himself from falling down thousands of feet below. Then, a park ranger on the edge of the cliff extends his hand in an attempt to pull him out of the precarious situation, but the rock climber is having trouble since he is holding on to his heavy bag and still does not want to let go of the useless items. This may sound ludicrous, because it is! We may think, why is the rock climber holding on to useless baggage? Let us ask ourselves a similar question. Why are we holding on to useless baggage on the inside? No need to revisit the garbage can. The items were placed there for a reason. Move on and let the healing begin.

10. <u>The Paradox of Healing</u>

There is an Eastern saying that states: 'Wherever the mind goes, energy flows.' Our mind is extremely powerful. A little thought is a dangerous thing. Objectively there are things that are simple, but subjectively we give meaning and form a specific relation to a particular situation or thing. If you are hurting because your boss rubbed you the wrong way or because your wife yelled at you then the objective reality is that it happened, but subjectively you can choose what to focus on, when to focus on the occurrence and how much time to spend on it. It is the analogy of taking a picture of a beautiful sunset. The picture taken without any filters is representative of the objective reality. The subjective experience kicks in when we crop the photo, click on the 'magic wand', embellish it and then finally we choose who we show the image to and also under what context. The feelings or emotional attachments to the picture are subjective. If we had a bad day and shared it with our friends then it may have twofold effects. To remember the incident since we needed someone to chat with in order to vent a little and blow off some steam is not a bad thing, but if we are doing it to seek pity in a selfish manner, then it can be detrimental. The more we bring up a negative occurrence to the mind the more we reinforce it in our minds and even create stronger connections to it in our brains as a physical reality. The more energy or thought in this case that we give it, the bigger the monster grows. Use the energy you have to be productive and channel the focus to people, places and goals that are actually worth your time. The less you care about something the less you should think of it. It is analogous to that of popularity with celebrities. Whether you like or dislike a particular celebrity is not relevant in this example. The fact of the matter is that the less people think about the person, the less likely it is that they will talk about the person, and the less likely it is that they will remember the person. Keeping a memory alive is like feeding it water and blasting it with sunlight and fertilizer. A little idea is indeed a dangerous thing. Wherever the mind goes energy flows toward it, making the thought bigger and stronger. So if you want to heal, do so not by continuously thinking about the occurrence that caused the hurt, but by focusing on other thoughts. Thus, comes the paradox of healing: If you want to move on, let it heal by not touching it. Time can heal wounds if you allow it to. We can only think of a few things at once; why not make them count? Face what you are feeling and do not seek to escape reality.

11. <u>The Escape Route</u>

Emotions are very powerful and cannot be underestimated. Oftentimes in our everyday lives we encounter particular difficulties that set off different emotions whether it be fear, anger or any deep passion. Although this may be the case, most times people cope with their feelings in a variety of ways. Some people may watch a movie to distract themselves from unpleasant feelings. Other people get a beer in an attempt to relax and to clear their mind. We all have mini escape routes so to speak. They can serve as healthy outlets, but we should never be emotionally attached to them. The moment we think that we need to find immediate pleasure in order to face everyday stress and see these escape routes as ends is the day that addictions begin. Paraphrasing Daniel Goleman's idea in "Emotional

Intelligence", there are grave cases when we feel as if we are drowning in stress or in a heap of difficulties and think that there is no way out, and then our mind goes into panic mode! Even before this stage becomes a reality, we must keep in mind to open up a psychological outlet. Open up a window or a door to let some psychological air circulate the room. No matter how bad a situation is that may spark an emotional meltdown there is ALWAYS a way out. Oftentimes our stress and intensity only add fuel to the flames. It is easier said than done, but staying calm and focused in an intense moment is vital to not losing one's peace. The ultimate positive escape route is to cling on to hope. Let us live intelligently. As long as we are still alive, the glimmer of hope stays alive with us.

12. <u>Social Intelligence</u>

Most of us have heard the modern buzz phrase of 'Emotional Intelligence'. An area which overlaps in the realms of IQ (Intelligence Quotient) and EQ (Emotional Quotient) is the SQ, or your 'Social Quotient'. Both emotions and intelligence interplay with social skills. Pragmatic societies sometimes place an exaggerated emphasis on intelligence and very practical skills that can generate wealth, but oftentimes people neglect the power of social prowess. Knowing what people want, need and how to relate to them are paramount skills. They are essential in business. If someone is a genius but cannot work well with others or is socially awkward, this could not only bring the mood down of the team, but even thwart the progress of a project. There is a social balance between being ourselves and being our adapted self and both are very important. People like to socialize with genuine people, but at the same time they do not want 'the full package' so to speak and prefer learned manners, social refinement and cultural protocols. The socially savvy individual knows how to be themselves and has the street smarts to know how and when to bend the expected social norms. We have a natural tendency to simply act out as we feel. This is especially true in little children since they have not developed any social filters that inhibit or curtail their natural selves. As time goes on we learn to curb our tongue, try to show interest in other people and develop certain social skills. Just like there are different types of trees and each seed grows from different conditions, the same applies to that of human beings. We do not live in a vacuum, so who we are is shaped by our experiences and who we interact with. It is the ongoing 'nature vs. nurture' debate. We may have the disposition of possessing innate social abilities, but if they are not practiced, then the person may not develop to their full potential. The reverse is true. Someone who may naturally be a bit awkward and shy might be able to improve given their social experiences, which help in chipping off the rough spots. There are many schools of thought, many different cultural dos and don'ts and even some social taboos, but below are some opinions on how to be more socially savvy.

1. Do not introduce yourself and then start asking a series of rapid fire questions like: 'What do you do for a living?' 'What is your position in the company?' In certain contextual social settings this may be somewhat permissible - for example, in a networking event where what you do is relevant to the purpose. However, in an open and casual social setting a question about what your profession is can

be awkward and lack social creativity. The reason being is that the person you ask might be unemployed. They might hate their job or be embarrassed about what they do. It might even be a very touchy subject. Another reason is that they might feel they are being compared to or sized up to see if they could fit inside their socially acceptable group. Someone who is socially savvy will talk about a fun hobby, about their recent vacation or what they did last weekend. From these stem a large network of other answers to some potential questions that you might have in a natural and nonthreatening way. Once the ice is broken and the person trusts you then they will naturally open up to you not only about what they do for a living but much more. If you start out by grilling a person with very personal questions, you will turn the person off and probably will not go much further.

2. Do not talk too much, especially about yourself. Even though you may be super interested in talking about your latest basket weaving competition, do not bore the person you are speaking to with all the details if they are not that interested. Read their body language as you are talking with them and see if they gauge any interest. When socializing, do not perform, but be yourself and be sure to read and interact. Anticipate giving the person an exit if you feel they are not interested or feel awkward about cutting the conversation short.

3. When socializing do not seek out any personal gain whatsoever. People can spot a phony from a mile away. Do not be an opportunist. If you are socializing and want to be a friend or even an acquaintance do not be ill intentioned and just seek out false friendships so that you can use them as stepping stones. If you are getting to know other people,

really try to get to know them and over time put them at ease so they know that you are not trying to 'sell' them anything.

4. Be yourself. If you are yourself it will be better for you and the other person. If you are fake you will attract fake friends and it will come back to haunt you.

5. Learn how to disagree without being disagreeable. Do not lack social tact by bluntly telling a person they are wrong. Ease it up a bit. Make sure you carry your message across with the least amount of harm. Put yourself in the shoes of the other person.

6. Do not be afraid of what others think of you. That is beyond your control. Have no fear.

13. <u>Fear</u>

Fear is a paralyzing emotion. Living in fear is like chaining yourself to a chair. You cannot move because of the shackles, yet with mental strength they can be broken. It has been said ad nauseum to 'not fear', 'to overcome your fears' and 'to fear not', but it depends what kind of fear. Fear is a defense mechanism. It is healthy to fear fire, wild animals, and steep cliffs. If we did not fear these things, then we may be in deep trouble. Fear in order to avoid disaster is not a bad thing, but the psychological fear of taking risks in life will kill your dreams. President FDR said that the "only thing we have to fear, is fear itself." It has also been popularly said that the word F.E.A.R. stands for 'false evidence appearing real.' Fear is good when it warns you of danger, but bad when it keeps you from moving ahead. It is good to have balance and measure, but at the same time not to be afraid of life. It is not good to never take any risks, and to take too many risks is crazy. We should take calculated risks. Most times people are too comfortable and are afraid of so many things that may never even happen to them. Paraphrasing Mark Twain he said that 'I've had a lot of worries in my life, most of which never happened.' A lot of our suffering comes from the anticipation of something bad happening and sometimes we worry about things that may never happen. If you feel deep inside your heart that you have a dream, a goal, a mission in your life - then go ahead and get it!

14. <u>If you feel ...</u>

If you feel PROUD, examine yourself, as you may be seeking a false platform for your ego.

If you feel ANGRY, examine if you are seeking revenge or desire evil on another person.

If you feel LUSTFUL, examine if your heart is in the right place and if you are acknowledging the dignity of other people.

If you feel LAZY, examine if you are grateful for your talents and if you appreciate the value of time.

If you feel GREEDY, examine if you are too attached to material goods and if you have a fear of the future.

If you feel JEALOUS, examine if you understand the purpose of your talents and if you have the right intentions for doing good works.

If you feel HEDONISTIC, examine if you understand the purpose of self-control and sobriety.

If you feel WORRIED, examine if you are living in the future, which does not exist.

If you feel SAD, examine if you are living in the past, which does not exist.

If you feel HAPPY, go ahead, and share your joy with the

others! There are way too many frowning faces in this

world. We cannot help everyone, but we make the world a

better place by helping to change one frown into a smile!

15. <u>Quotes to Ponder on</u>

"Successful people don't necessarily make less mistakes than everyone else. In fact, they probably make more mistakes and have their emotional meltdowns, but the difference is that successful people are constantly learning from each mistake."

"Failure happens when you let your emotions guide your reason. Success happens when reason guides your emotions."

"Giving in to your emotions is like honking your horn during traffic. It doesn't fix the problem, and no one wants to hear it."

"If you remain strong during your weakest moment you are not only helping yourself, but everyone else around you."

"Emotions are like nuclear energy: they can provide useful power or destruction; the choice is yours!"

"If you don't control your emotions, they will control you. Once the emotions take possession of one's mind, it's game over."

"Don't let your feelings win. Fight once more especially when you're tired, sore and have nothing left in your system. It's these moments that define your true character."

"There is a balance between feelings and facts. Don't seek to feel good, but to be good. Don't seek to be liked, but be likeable. If you disagree, don't be disagreeable."

"Sometimes no words are needed to provide motivation. It's all about connecting to the heart. If someone has the power to open your heart it is up to you to take advantage of that moment to follow your calling."

"Your drive can't be based on feelings. If the world is against you, remember that no one on earth can stop you from fulfilling your ultimate mission in life."

"Don't let your feelings drown you when the tide is high. The more difficult a situation is, the more room there is for potential growth."

"Even though you may not know the road with clarity, you can't fail down the path of charity. We need to acknowledge that love surpasses knowledge."

"Channel your emotions no matter how small. The little things will either make or break you."

"Don't give me the excuse that you lack drive. Go beyond your feelings and simply choose to be motivated. To learn how to run you can't wonder about it; you have to start moving those legs."

"Nobody cares about your hurt ego. Just let it go. If you are humiliated, it's an opportunity to grow in humility."

"Success comes down to sticking to your game plan when you absolutely don't feel like it and when you think it makes 'no sense' to continue."

"A good worker sees opportunities when business is running smoothly, but a great worker, regardless of the feelings and circumstances, only sees opportunities."

"Lack of emotional balance may cause insecurities. If you are trying to prove yourself, you will only prove that you are insecure. If you are seeking out the good of the others, then you will find the security that you lack."

"People may not remember your fancy presentation with all the numbers, charts and statistics, but they will remember how you made them feel. Business comes down to: 'Can I trust you?'"

"If the world praises you, don't let your head swell. If the world mocks you, don't let your heart shrink."

"If you can control your emotions, fear not the outcome of the battles you are about to face; if you can't, then you're already defeated."

"Being enraptured by your emotions is like an army marching through a thick fog. Have patience until it clears out, lest your troops should fall into a ditch."

"A way to find your passion is to first acknowledge what interests or hobbies you naturally gravitate towards regardless of whether or not it brings any financial or professional prestige."

"If you're chasing money you may never find your passion. If you're chasing your passion you may never find your money. If you're good at what you're passionate about and the world needs it, then the money will soon follow."

"You always end up defeated when you get angry because your heart becomes a slave to your emotions."

"Sometimes just your presence is all that your friend needs at the moment."

"We give meaning to our meaningless tasks by the love that we put into them."

"If you lack resources, you are limited for a moment, but if you lack motivation you are limited for a lifetime."

"We may have been rejected, criticized, beaten, humiliated and emotionally destroyed, but don't give up. These are all opportunities to learn and grow."

"A burst of enthusiasm may be needed at the moment, but perseverance is needed in the long run."

"When you are angry, wait patiently until you cool off. Once the heat has subsided you can react with greater strength and finesse."

"Your world of 'I can't' will make you powerless, yet the power of your 'I will' can change the world."

"If you genuinely love what you do, then you will never lose your motivation. Doing what you love is its own reward."

"If your feelings overwhelm you, don't let them break you down but have them break you, open to a new beginning."

"Feelings may come and go, but never lose your motivation."

"Emotions may give you a boost, but you need discipline to keep moving forward."

"In order to have peace, we must piece our life in order."

"Don't regret not having done what you loved so much as not having loved as you ought."

"Smile often. Enjoy life. Be yourself. Fear nothing. Love always!"